IS-775: EOC Management and Operations

By

Fema

8/6/2008

Lesson 1: Introduction and Course Overview

Course Welcome

Welcome to the **EOC Management and Operations** online course. This course will prepare Emergency Management Coordinators, senior officials, key EOC personnel, and others to function more effectively in an EOC environment.

After taking this course, you should be able to assess your jurisdiction's EOC facility and setup. You should also be able to determine whether your systems and staffing are adequate for your jurisdiction's needs. Finally, you should be able to determine tests, training, and exercises required to evaluate your EOC's operations.

Lesson Objectives

At the completion of this lesson, you should be able to:

- Describe the course purposes.
- Describe the role of the EOC.

The Role of the EOC

The EOC provides a central location from which government at any level can provide interagency **coordination** and executive **decisionmaking** in support of the incident response.

The EOC does not command or control the on-scene response. The EOC carries out the **coordination** function through:

- Information collection and evaluation.
- Priority setting.
- Resource management.

Decisionmaking at the EOC affects the incident response as well as the public response. The decisions made at the EOC are not tactical decisions, however. Tactical decisions are made by the Incident Commander and the Command Staff at the incident scene.

- The EOC may be the facility from which the multiple agencies or organizations involved are coordinated.
- The EOC also plays a critical role in support of the on-scene response.

This course will cover the most significant aspects of EOC management and operations.

Lesson 2: EOCs and Multiagency Coordination

Lesson Objectives

At the completion of this lesson, you should be able to:

- Relate EOC operations to National Incident Management System (NIMS) requirements.
- Describe the role that EOCs play in overall multiagency coordination.
- Describe the relationship between the EOC and the on-scene Incident Command System (ICS) organization.
- List the key factors for an effective EOC operation.

EOCs—The Critical Link in Emergency Response

EOCs coordinate with on-scene incident managers and other agencies and organizations to:

- Acquire, allocate, and track resources.
- Manage and share information.
- Establish response priorities among incidents.
- Provide legal and financial support.
- Liaison with other jurisdictions and other levels of government.

Jurisdictions with well-organized EOCs have several distinct advantages over other jurisdictions during an emergency because they:

- Serve as a conduit for information passed from the incident scene, through lower-level coordination agencies, to higher-level coordination entities.
- Allow the Incident Commander to focus on managing the incident.
- Promote problem resolution at the lowest practical level.
- Provide strategic guidance and direction to support incident management activities.

EOCs and NIMS

EOCs are part of a larger system of **multiagency coordination** that is integral to domestic response as required by the National Incident Management System (NIMS).

NIMS is a flexible response framework that is applicable to all hazards and jurisdictions.

NIMS represents a core set of **doctrine, concepts, principles, terminology,** and **organizational processes** that enables effective, efficient, and collaborative incident management.

NIMS is **not:**

- An operational incident management plan.
- A resource allocation plan.
- A terrorism-specific plan.
- An international plan.

NIMS Components

NIMS—a nationwide, systematic approach to domestic incident management—consists of five components:

- Preparedness.
- Communications and Information Management.
- Resource Management.
- Command and Management.
- Ongoing Management and Maintenance.

Preparedness

Effective incident management begins with a host of preparedness activities conducted on a "steady-state" basis, well in advance of any potential incident. Preparedness involves an integrated combination of planning, training, exercises, personnel qualification and certification standards, and equipment certification.

Communications and Information Management

Emergency management and incident response activities rely on communications and information management systems that provide a common operating picture to all command and coordination sites. NIMS describes the requirements for a standardized framework for communications and emphasizes the need for a common operating picture. NIMS is based on the concepts of **interoperability, reliability, scalability, portability,** and **resiliency and redundancy** of communications and information systems.

Resource Management

Resources—personnel, equipment, and/or supplies—are needed to support critical incident objectives. The flow of resources must be fluid and adaptable to the requirements of the incident. NIMS defines standardized mechanisms and establishes the resource management process to identify requirements; order and acquire resources; mobilize, track, and report resource status; recover and demobilize resources; reimburse for resource use; and inventory resources.

Command and Management

The Command and Management component within NIMS is designed to enable effective and efficient incident management and coordination by providing a flexible, standardized incident management structure. The structure is based on three organizational constructs:

- The Incident Command System (ICS). ICS defines the operating characteristics, interactive management components, and structure of incident management and emergency response organizations engaged throughout the life cycle of an incident. NIMS requires government officials to:
    - Adopt NIMS through executive order, proclamation, or legislation as the jurisdiction's official incident management system.
    - Direct incident managers and response organizations in their jurisdictions to train, exercise, and use ICS for all incidents and planned events, including the development of Incident Action Plans (IAPs) and Common Communications Plans (CCPs).
    - Integrate ICS into functional and systemwide emergency operations policies, plans, and procedures.
    - Conduct ICS training for responders, supervisors, and command-level officers.
    - Conduct coordinating ICS-oriented exercises that involve responders from multiple disciplines and jurisdictions.
- Multiagency Coordination Systems (MACS). MACS define the operating characteristics, interactive management components, and organizational structure of supporting incident management entities engaged at the Federal, State, local, tribal, and regional levels through mutual-aid agreements and other assistance arrangements. MACS include a combination of facilities, equipment, personnel, and procedures integrated into a common system with responsibility for coordination of resources and support to emergency operations.

    The primary functions of MACS are to coordinate activities above the field level and to prioritize incident demands for critical or competing resources. For the purpose of coordinating resources, MACS can be implemented from a fixed facility—such as an EOC—or by other arrangements outlined within the system.
- Public Information. Public Information refers to processes, procedures, and systems for communicating timely and accurate information to the public during crisis or emergency situations.

Ongoing Management and Maintenance

Within the Ongoing Management and Maintenance component of NIMS, there are two subsections:

- The National Integration Center. The National Integration Center (NIC) Incident Management Systems Division was established by the Secretary of Homeland Security to provide "strategic direction for and oversight of the National Incident Management System (NIMS)... supporting both routine maintenance and the continuous refinement of the system and its components over the long term." The Center oversees all aspects of NIMS including the development of compliance criteria and implementation activities at Federal, State, and local levels. It provides guidance and support to jurisdictions and incident management and responder organizations as they adopt the system.

  The Center is a multidisciplinary entity made up of Federal stakeholders and, over time, it will include representatives of State, local, and tribal incident management and responder organizations. It is situated within the Department of Homeland Security's Federal Emergency Management Agency.
- Supporting Technologies. Technology and technological systems provide supporting capabilities essential to implement and continuously refine NIMS. These include voice and data communications systems, information management systems (i.e., recordkeeping and resource tracking), and data display systems. Also included are specialized technologies that facilitate ongoing operations and incident management activities in situations that call for unique technology-based capabilities.

EOC Functions

EOCs serve several main functions within a MACS:

- **Information collection and evaluation**—collecting, analyzing, and interpreting information from various sources.
- **Coordination**—coordinating the information flow and resources for complex incidents or multiple incidents occurring simultaneously.
- **Priority setting**—ensuring that response systems are interconnected and complementary, reinforcing interoperability among the various system components, making response more efficient and effective by coordinating available resources, and making decisions based on agreed-upon policies and procedures.
- **Resource coordination**—identifying and acquiring needed resources and allocating existing or known resources.
- **Communications facilitation**—establishing interoperable communications among all partners in the MACS and others, as necessary for the response.

EOCs and Multiagency Coordination Systems

Most emergencies are handled by first responders, fire, law enforcement, and emergency medical personnel; but in a large emergency or disaster, the efforts of first response agency personnel and others must be coordinated to ensure an effective response.

In these situations, Emergency Operations Centers (EOCs) play a critical role in acquiring, allocating and tracking resources, managing and distributing information, and setting response priorities among many incident sites.

EOCs are a critical link in the emergency response chain, enabling incident commanders to focus on the needs of the incident, serving as a conduit of information between the incident command and higher levels of MAC system entities, and promoting problem solving at the lowest practical level.

EOCs are part of the larger Multi-Agency Coordination System that is integral to the National Incident Management System (NIMS). NIMS is a flexible framework of doctrine, concepts, principles, terminology, and organizational processes that is applicable to all hazards and jurisdictions.

NIMS integrates existing best practices into a consistent nationwide approach to domestic incident management.

Effective Multi-Agency Coordination helps in establishing response priorities and allocating resources, resolving differences among agencies, and providing strategic guidance and direction.

Multi-Agency Coordination is a system, not a facility. Entities that may comprise a multi-agency system include dispatch, on-scene command, resource coordination centers, emergency operations centers, and coordination entities in groups.

As part of the overall MAC system, the EOC provides a central location where government at any level can provide interagency coordination and executive decision making in support of the incident response.

This course will help you manage and operate your EOC to help ensure a safe, efficient, and effective response to any incident.

EOC Purpose

Remember, the purpose of an EOC is to establish a central location where government at any level can provide interagency coordination and execute decisionmaking to support incident response.

Incidents are best managed at the lowest possible level:

- Geographically.
- Organizationally.
- Jurisdictionally.

Local EOCs provide resource coordination and support to the on-scene Incident Command. When local resources are exceeded, State EOCs may provide additional expertise, resources, and support.

When State resources are exceeded, State EOCs may request additional resource support and coordination assistance from other States or from the Federal Government.

EOC Benefits

An effective EOC:

- Helps establish a common operating picture.
- Facilitates long-term operations.
- Improves continuity.
- Provides ready access to all available information.
- Simplifies information analysis and verification.
- Promotes resource identification and assignment.

A single EOC facility functions more efficiently. With a single location, officials can meet, make decisions, and coordinate activities.

ICS/EOC Relationships

Incident Commanders have several critical needs with which EOC personnel can assist. These needs include:

- **A common operating picture**—critical during incidents that are large or complex, or involve personnel from multiple response agencies.

- **Policy direction**—critical when jurisdictions with differing policies are involved in a response.
- **Communication support**—critical in large, complex incidents or when multiple jurisdictions are involved in a response.
- **Resources**—includes people, equipment, and supplies required for a response.
- **Strategic planning**—allows the Incident Commander to focus on tactics.
- **Legal and financial support**—frees on-scene resources to focus on the response.

EOCs can help meet the needs at the incident scene by:

- **Providing the "big picture"** view of the incident.
- **Establishing policy** or resolving conflicting policies.
- **Providing communications** and messaging support.
- **Managing public information** issues and media requests.
- **Providing and prioritizing resources.**
- **Authorizing emergency expenditures,** when appropriate, and tracking incident costs.

Factors for an Effective EOC

To ensure effective EOC operations, focus on:

- The facility.
- Equipment.
- Personnel.
- Procedures.

Consider these factors when selecting an EOC or alternate EOC, when designing a floor plan for the EOC, or when evaluating EOC operations. These factors will be covered in more depth in subsequent lessons.

Lesson 3: EOC Staffing and Organization

Lesson Objectives

At the completion of this lesson, you should be able to:

- Identify key EOC operations for your jurisdiction.
- Determine staff to meet the requirements of key EOC operations.
- Describe four ways to organize the EOC staff.
- Select the EOC organization that best meets your jurisdiction's operational requirements.

EOC Staffing: Factors To Consider

There are several key factors to consider when staffing the EOC.

What must be done?	The tasks to be performed are **the critical driver** for EOC staffing. Identifying the tasks will point to the staff needed.
What is the timeframe?	Extended operations fuel a need for alternate and support staff for 24/7 coverage.
Who has the knowledge, skills, and abilities to perform critical tasks?	All personnel must have the knowledge, skills, and abilities required for the duties assigned. If training or cross-training is necessary, it **must** occur as part of the planning cycle.
Who has the authority to make critical decisions?	All persons assigned to the EOC must have the authority to do what is required by their jobs.

Each of these factors will be further described in this section.

What Must Be Done?

Begin by considering essential functions to be performed at the EOC. Proper identification of essential functions is critical for effective EOC operations. Other aspects of the EOC are designed around these functions.

If an essential function is not properly identified, there will be no arrangements to perform that function.

On the other hand, identifying too many functions as essential can lead to confusion during EOC operations.

What Is the Timeframe?

The possibility of extended operations will drive second- and/or third-shift personnel, backup personnel, and support personnel needs for EOC operations.

- **Alternate staff assignments** are necessary during extended operations so all positions are staffed 24/7.
- **Support staff** is necessary to assist with critical tasks or to perform support tasks, such as trash collection, food preparation and cleanup, administrative tasks, maintenance, etc.

Who Has the Knowledge, Skills, and Abilities To Perform Critical Tasks?

When considering EOC staffing, look at:

- **Knowledge** of the critical tasks involved in performing the function.
- **Skills** required to perform the tasks.
- The **ability** to:
    - Work under pressure.
    - Interact well with others.
    - Work extended hours, if necessary.

Who Has the Authority To Make Critical Decisions?

Ensuring that all personnel have the authority to perform the tasks assigned is of paramount importance.

For example …

- Many people may have the knowledge, skills, and ability to **manage** a contract, few have the authority to **execute** a contract.
- Most staff **have an opinion** of what policy to implement, few have the **authority to enact** policy.

The best way to ensure that EOC staff are authorized to perform their essential functions is to predelegate authorities for enacting policy or making decisions. Most agencies routinely use delegations of authority so decisions can be made in the absence of key decisionmakers.

Delegations of Authority:

- Take effect when an emergency occurs that requires EOC activation or when normal channels of direction and control are disrupted.
- Terminate when the emergency ends or when normal channels of direction and control are restored.

During an emergency situation, Delegations of Authority:

- Effect a rapid response.
- Establish a clear chain of command.

Orders of Succession

All agencies activated for EOC operations need **Orders of Succession** in place. Orders of succession take effect when government or agency leaders are incapacitated or unavailable in an emergency requiring EOC activation.

Orders of succession should be sufficiently in depth (at least three deep) to ensure an agency can continue managing and directing its operations while remaining viable during an emergency.

Staffing to Support Essential Functions

Essential functions must continue, even with reduced staffing. Plan for training and cross-training of all EOC staff:

- Some primary staff may be injured or may not be available.
- Transportation routes to the EOC may be disrupted, prohibiting primary staff from reaching the facility.

All personnel must be trained for their jobs in the EOC. As a contingency, specific staff should be cross-trained to ensure that EOC operations can continue with a smaller number of staff than originally planned.

Organizing the EOC Staff

NIMS requires all jurisdictions to adopt ICS as its incident management system. NIMS does **not** require EOCs to adopt ICS as their organizational structure. An EOC should be organized to facilitate **effective** operations.

An effective organization has these characteristics:

- Ability to acquire, analyze, and act on information.
- Flexibility in the face of rapidly changing conditions.
- Ability to anticipate change.
- Ability to maintain public confidence.
- Reliability over time.

An EOC should be organized to maximize each of the characteristics of an effective organization.

EOC Organizations

There are typically four ways to organize EOCs:

Each of these organization structures has advantages and disadvantages. In some cases, the structure selected depends on State law. In other cases, the structure simply is the one that works best for the jurisdiction.

Each of these organization structures is described next.

Organizing by Major Management Activities

The **Policy Group** is comprised of the Chief Elected Official, or designee, and immediate staff. The Policy Group focuses on the overall strategy for the response (beyond the strategy developed by the Incident Commander at the scene), the overall response priorities, and policy setting. Decisions made by the Policy Group are implemented by the Coordination, Operations, and Resource Groups.

The **Resource Group** should include representatives from any agency or organization that is providing—or may be requested to provide—resources for the response. These agencies or organizations may include transportation agencies, utility companies, representatives of business and industry, mutual aid partners, and others.

The **Operations Group** should include representatives from each agency with responsibility for any portion of the response. Units within the Operations Group may include law enforcement, fire, public works, emergency medical services, and other agencies, as dictated by the incident.

The **Coordination Group** collects and analyzes data, including damage data and damage prediction data.

Advantages and disadvantages of organizing by major management activities are shown below.

Advantages	Disadvantages
Organization is relatively simple, with straightforward lines of communication and chain of command.	**Linkages with the ICS organization on-scene may be unclear at times because there is not a one-to-one match between the incident organization and the EOC organization.**
All key decisionmakers and representatives of participating agencies are included, as appropriate, within the organization, and all can contribute as needed.	**There may be confusion about who does resource ordering, the Operations Group or the Resources Group.**

Despite the potential coordination issue, many jurisdictions have used this structure successfully.

Organizing Around ICS

The EOC **Command** function is **not** the Incident Commander. The Incident Commander or Unified Command are on-scene command structures. The EOC Command function serves a similar role to the Policy Group and makes decisions that establish the overall strategy of the response.

The **Operations** function has responsibility for coordinating with and supporting on-scene responders. Branches, Divisions, and Groups assigned to the Operations function can be organized as necessary to support the incident(s).

The **Planning** function serves the same purpose as at the incident scene—gathering and analyzing information, keeping decisionmakers informed, and tracking resources. Technical Specialists may be assigned to the Planning function or may be assigned elsewhere, as needed.

The **Logistics** function also serves the same purpose as at the incident scene, frequently serving as the single ordering point for the incident(s) in its purview, providing overall communications planning for the jurisdiction, coordinating transportation and housing, etc.

The **Finance/Administration** function provides a coordinated financial management process for the incident(s) in its purview.

The advantages and disadvantages of using an ICS organization in the EOC are shown in the table below.

Advantages	Disadvantages
Clarity of roles and functional integrity. The ICS organization in the field has a clear contact point in the EOC.	**Potential for confusion about command authority at the incident scene versus in the EOC.**
Large incident logistical and financial support is often coordinated more easily from the EOC and may relieve the workload on incident and dispatch staff.	**No disadvantages**

Many jurisdictions have used this structure successfully.

Organizing by ESF

This EOC organization structure is based on the Emergency Support Functions (ESFs) of the National Response Framework. The Command and General Staff have descriptors similar to the ICS model. ESFs are assigned under each General Staff position.

The **Operations** area includes:

- Public Works/Emergency Engineering Branch.
- Firefighting Branch.
- Public Health and Medical Services Branch.
- Urban Search and Rescue Branch.
- Public Safety/Law Enforcement Branch.

The **Planning** area includes:

- Situation Analysis Unit.
- Documentation Unit.
- Advanced Planning Unit.

- Technical Services Unit.
- Damage Assessment.
- Resource Status Unit.
- GIS.

The **Logistics** area includes:

- Situation Analysis Unit.
- Communications Unit.
- Food Unit.
- Medical Unit.
- Transportation Unit.
- Supply Unit.
- Facilities Unit.

The **Finance/Administration** area includes:

- Compensation Claims Unit
- Cost Unit.
- Purchasing/Procurement Unit.
- Time Unit.
- Disaster Financial Assistance.

The advantages and disadvantages of organizing the EOC by ESF are shown in the table below.

Advantages	Disadvantages
Coordinates well with on-scene ICS organizations, therefore appeals to local and State EOCs.	**State and/or local ESFs may not correspond directly with Federal ESFs and do not correspond directly with the ICS positions in the on-scene Operations Section.**
Provides a clear one-to-one relationship with the National Response Framework.	**Organizing by ESF requires an enormous amount of additional training to ensure that the agencies responsible for ESFs are able to perform their duties.**

Many jurisdictions have used this structure successfully.

Organizing as a MAC Group

A **MAC Group** is made up of organization, agency, or jurisdiction representatives who are authorized to commit agency resources and funds. The success of the MAC Group depends on its membership. Sometimes membership is obvious—organizations that are directly impacted and whose resources are committed to the incident.

Often, organizations that should be members of a MAC Group are less obvious. These organizations may include the local Chamber of Commerce, volunteer organizations, the American Red Cross, or other organizations with special expertise or knowledge.

While these agencies may not have "hard" resources or funds to contribute, their contacts, political influence, or technical expertise may be key to the success of the MAC Group.

The **MAC Group Coordinator** is an optional position to provide supervision to the various units.

The results of the MAC Group's deliberation are distributed by its members directly to their organizations as well as through the normal chain of command (MAC Entities, Dispatch Centers, etc.).

The **MAC Group Situation Assessment Unit** collects and assembles information needed for the MAC Group to fulfill its mission.

The **MAC Group Resource Status Information Unit** collects and assembles information needed for the MAC Group to fulfill its mission.

The **Joint Information Center (JIC)** is a Public Information Unit that coordinates summary information and access to local information sources in the media and other governmental entities.

The advantages and disadvantages of organizing the EOC as a MAC Group are shown in the table below.

Advantages	Disadvantages
Works well to ensure coordination among other MAC Entities.	**Lacks clearly defined, standardized relationships to other MAC Entities, since it is a "generic" MAC Entity that can be used at any level of government. Each MAC Group must carefully define its relationship to the EOC, JIC, etc.**

Useful when a mechanism is needed to provide short-term multiagency coordination and decisionmaking where no such mechanism exists. It can be incorporated into existing EOC structures as the policymaking part of the organization.	**No associated implementation staff, which makes it difficult to use as a stand-alone EOC structure.**

Lesson 4: Determining Communications Needs

Lesson Objectives

At the completion of this lesson, you should be able to:

- Describe the NIMS requirements for communications.
- Develop a communications map to identify who needs to communicate with whom during an emergency.
- Identify primary and backup means of communicating among key personnel, both on-scene and within the MACS.

NIMS Requirements for Communications

NIMS has established two basic requirements for communications:

- Interoperability.
- Redundancy.

Each of these requirements will be described on the screens that follow.

Interoperability

Many jurisdictions believe that their communications systems are interoperable but, when in a wide-scale emergency or disaster, interoperability problems emerge.

Interoperability Issues

The results of two surveys point to interoperability problems:

Only 6 of 75 of the largest U.S. metropolitan areas received the highest interoperability ratings.
(*Tactical Interoperable Communications Scorecards Summary Report and Findings, January 2007*)

Emergency workers from only 2/3 of 6,800 communities surveyed claim that they can talk to each other on a routine basis.
(*2006 National Interoperability Baseline Survey, December 2006*)

Interoperability Factors

The ability for first responders, and those who support them, to communicate with each other is a long-standing issue.

Interoperability—the ability for public safety agencies to exchange voice and/or data on demand and in real time—has been pointed to as an issue in emergencies as diverse as hurricanes and floods, earthquakes, and terrorist attacks.

Lack of redundant interoperable communications can delay a response, making even the most urgent response inefficient, and ultimately costly to those lives who cannot be saved.

Why is interoperability such a difficult issue to solve? Recent studies have identified five key reasons for lack of interoperability—aging or incompatible communications infrastructure, limited funding to update or replace equipment, coupled with different funding priorities and budget cycles, limited and fragmented planning, the reluctance of agencies to give up control over their communication systems, and limited and fragmented radio spectrum availability.

The communication infrastructure in many jurisdictions is antiquated. Old equipment means higher maintenance costs, reduced reliability, and obsolescence for public safety agencies. ,Many systems in use today are obsolete or will become obsolete as manufacturer support is discontinued.

Some newer digital communications systems lack interoperability with other systems because of proprietary software. Additionally standards for technology and equipment are limited.

There is limited funding to replace and update communications equipment, and different communities and levels of government have different funding schedules and budget priorities. Additionally, regulations in one jurisdiction may conflict with those in another.

Funding is often stove piped to meet individual agency needs, and spending decisions may be based on old strategies that did not consider the need for interoperability.

Planning for interoperability remains limited and fragmented. Without adequate planning, time and money can be wasted, and end results could be disappointing. Competition among agencies, jurisdictions, and different levels of government inhibit the partnerships and leadership required to develop interoperability.

Interoperability requires a certain amount of shared management, control, and coordination of policy and procedures. Agencies are, naturally, reluctant to give up management and control of their communications systems.

Finally, as public safety agencies share radio frequencies with television and radio, government users, and commercial users, the amount of radio spectrum available to public safety agencies has become fragmented.

Advancing technology is placing greater requirements on radio spectrum, making it more scarce and more valuable at a time when public safety agencies need additional spectrum to support emerging technologies.

So how can your public safety agencies, your jurisdiction, and your State improve its communications interoperability? First determine your current level of interoperability. After determining where you are, you can work on what you need and how to get it. This unit will help you with each of these steps.

Determining Interoperability

To determine the level of interoperability, consider these questions:

Who needs to communicate?	Identify communications requirements by function or position, not by name.
With whom does he/she need to communicate?	Consider communications needs both inside and outside of the EOC.
What information must be communicated?	Consider routine information, priority information, and classified or sensitive information.
What means of communication will be used?	Consider all possible types of communication (e.g., radio, telephone, fax, runner).

Making these determinations requires in-depth, position-by-position analysis of the MACS, from the Incident Command Post through the Federal level of government (in the case of Presidentially declared disasters or emergencies).

Mapping EOC Communications

Answer the communications questions by mapping necessary communications for each function or position within the EOC. A communications "map" **needs** to answer the questions:

- **Who?**
- **What?**
- **When?**
- **How?**

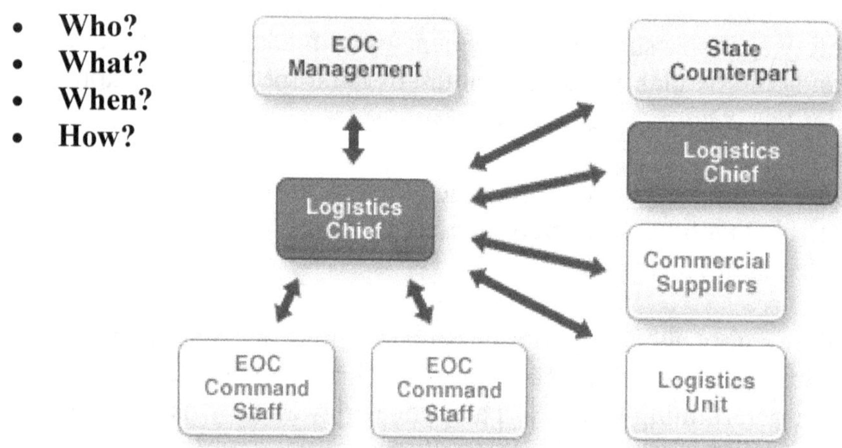

Interoperability can be addressed only after these questions are answered. Communications must flow from the incident scene through the highest level of the MACS required for the response.

Determining Interoperability—Radio Communications

Radio remains the primary communications method in most jurisdictions. Since radio communications systems are expensive to purchase or update, jurisdictions need to be able to assess their current radio communications capability.

Factors Affecting Radio Communications

Factors that affect radio communications include:

- Geography and topography.
- Presence of high-rise buildings or other concrete and/or steel structures.
- Frequencies allocated to emergency communications.
- Incompatible systems.

These are a few of the many factors that affect the ability of one agency to communicate with another by radio. Other factors that stretch beyond system capabilities include:

- The failure of response agencies to communicate in "plain English."
- Multiple dispatch centers that necessitate relaying information between response agencies.
- Political issues.

Redundancy

What will you do if your primary communications system fails?

Much of the communications infrastructure in the Gulf Coast region was heavily damaged or destroyed by Hurricane Katrina, making emergency communications difficult or impossible for some period of time.

Having redundant systems in place and ensuring that all agencies involved in a response know what those systems are and how they will be notified to switch to the backup system may be critical to maintaining communications.

The EOC will likely be responsible for implementing backup communications systems and notifying personnel to switch to the backup system.

Redundancy Summary

Remember…

All agencies assisting in a response need to switch to a backup system when required.	Even agencies that are infrequent players (e.g., the public health agency) need the communications capability that backup systems provide.
A system may work in one situation but not in another.	Multiple backup systems should be planned and exercised. Procedures for switching to the backup systems are needed to ensure that everyone who needs to communicate can.
Backup systems must accommodate secure communications where necessary.	Operational information must be protected from widespread dissemination.

Communicating with the Media

Don't forget public information!

Some members of the media will go to great lengths for a story. It just makes good sense to provide the media with the information they—and the public—need.

NIMS requires public information be organized around a **Joint Information System (JIS)** that is overseen by a **Public Information Officer (PIO).**

Public Information should consider:

- Who is the public?
- What does the public need to know?
- Who will provide that information?
- Who will manage the information flow?
- How will the information be transmitted?
- When?
- How often?

The answers to these questions will determine how the JIS is established and how it will operate.

Using Public Information as Input to Leaders

Public Information also provides critical information to elected officials, agency administrators, and responders. For example, elected officials and others can tell a lot about whether their message is effective by monitoring:

- Whether the public is responding appropriately to warnings and emergency messages.
- Rumors that are circulating.

The JIS should be designed to monitor incoming information as well as outgoing information.

Benefits of a Well-Developed Joint Information System

The JIS is an organized, integrated, and coordinated mechanism for delivery of **understandable, timely, accurate, and consistent** information to the public during an emergency.

The JIS includes the **plans, protocols, and structures** used to provide information to the public during incident operations.

The JIS encompasses all public information operations related to the incident:

- Federal
- State
- Local
- Tribal
- Private organization PIOs
- Staff
- JICs established to support the incident

JIS Key Elements:

- Interagency coordination and integration
- Development and delivery of coordinated messages
- Support for decisionmakers
- Flexibility, modularity, and adaptability

The Public Information Officer

The Public Information Officer (PIO) represents and advises the Incident Command.

Through the JIS, the PIO coordinates:

- Media and public inquiries.
- Emergency public information and warnings.
- Rumor monitoring and response.
- Media monitoring.

Through the EOC, the PIO ensures that the media and, therefore, the public receive a consistent message in a timely manner.

Lesson 5: Determining Information, Systems, and Equipment Needs

Lesson Objectives

At the completion of this lesson, you should be able to:

- Identify the information needs for EOC operations.
- Determine the systems and equipment required to support the EOC staff's information needs.

Information Management: Questions To Answer

Before you can manage information, you need to determine:

- What information do you need?
- What will you do with it?
- How will you protect it?
- How will you preserve it?

Types of Information

The types of information managed in the EOC fall into two categories:

Emergency operating records include records, regardless of media, that are essential to EOC operations and response support.

Legal and financial records include records, regardless of media, that are critical to carrying out the legal and financial responsibilities for the response.

Identifying and Reviewing Required Information

Identify the information needed during EOC operations by compiling a detailed list of the records. This list needs to be reviewed and updated routinely, at least on an annual basis.

Other events that should trigger a review include:

- **Change in the jurisdiction.** Personnel changes necessitate changes to orders of succession, delegations of authority, call-down rosters, and other records.
- **EOC activation.** After-action reports document the information needed to support incident response.

Maintaining Information

Many of these information types are maintained electronically. Training, testing, and exercise procedures should ensure that personnel can access the records in an emergency.

Specific procedures to achieve this capability depend on the nature of the information and the system used to store, retrieve, process, and report the information.

Meeting Information Needs

How you **use** information will determine how you **manage** it. Look at the information used, how it is used, and by whom it is used to determine whether your current management strategy is the best available.

Information Use	Information Management Strategy
Information many people need access to or Information that is used at several different locations	Provide easy access, allowing for ease of update and sharing. Version control is critical for this information.
Secure or classified information	Secure storage access and are critical considerations for this type of information.
Information transmitted to the public	Provide ready accessibility to those with authority to speak to the media. This information **must** be kept current.

Providing Information to Key Personnel

During an incident, key personnel rely on timely, accurate information. An effective operation at the EOC requires access to **all** of the information needed to make good, timely decisions. Key personnel must have access to:

- Email.
- All information that they would have at the incident scene or at department headquarters.
- Operational data from departmental or other databases.
- Information needed from other key personnel throughout the MACS.

Providing Information for Support Personnel

Support personnel have the need for:

- Static files that are maintained in the EOC.
- Dynamic files that are maintained by the jurisdiction or individual agencies (police, fire, etc.) or created at the EOC during each emergency.
- "Go" kits that are maintained by individuals or individual agencies.

Static files are unchanging or change infrequently. Examples of static files are policies and procedures, delegations of authority, and jurisdiction maps.

Dynamic files change frequently or are unique to the emergency. Examples of dynamic files are resource assignments and agency call-down rosters.

An office **"Go" kit** is a briefcase (or similar container) holding information and supplies the owner will need in an emergency. Common items included in "Go" kits are:

- Office supplies.
- Maps.
- SOPs and other directives.
- Spare cell phone and computer batteries.

Meeting Information Needs

Addressing information needs is part of the emergency planning process. Documentation for each function in the EOC operation should include:

- The information needed.

- Who needs the information.
- How the information will be used.
- How the information will be stored, updated, and maintained.
- How the information will be recovered if damaged or lost.

Meeting the Public's Information Needs

The public also has information needs. The Joint Information System (JIS) must include:

- Protocols for coordinating information dissemination to the public.
- Templates for key communications, such as warnings, public-service announcements (PSAs), and other emergency information.
- A Joint Information Center (JIC) as a central location for disseminating information to the media.
- Staff at the JIC trained as Public Information Officers (PIOs).

Agency PIOs should use JIS procedures to coordinate information flow and dissemination with the incident PIO. This ensures an accurate, consistent message to the public.

Determining Equipment and System Needs

Equipment and systems are needed to support information requirements. The equipment and systems required depends on:

- Who stores and maintains the information.
- How the information is stored and maintained.
- How many people need to access the information at any given time.
- How often the information changes or requires updating.
- How sensitive the information is.

Lesson 6: Designing the EOC

Lesson Objectives

At the completion of this lesson, you should be able to:

- Analyze your current EOC facilities for functionality.
- Articulate the need for an alternate EOC and describe the minimum requirements for the alternate facility.

EOC Location Factors

The main factors involved in locating an EOC are:

- Accessibility
- Safety
- Size
- Systems Capability
- Survivability
- Versatility

Accessibility: Areas To Consider

When considering accessibility, there are two main areas of concern:

1. **Can key personnel get to the EOC within the required timeframe?** The timeframe required for key personnel to report will vary depending on the type, size, and complexity of the emergency. The EOC location should be **immediately** accessible, regardless of the emergency.

2. **Can suppliers and support personnel get to the EOC without delay, when needed?** Operations lasting more than one operational period will require second-shift personnel. Larger, more complex emergencies will require additional EOC personnel. Long-term operations may require supplier support for delivery of supplies or vendor support to make repairs.

Changes in population, highway access, and other factors necessitate periodic review of EOC accessibility.

Accessibility: EOC Location Factors

Review your jurisdiction's hazard/vulnerability analysis periodically to determine whether:

The EOC is accessible regardless of hazard.	Locate EOC so that it will be relatively unaffected by the jurisdiction's high-risk, high-probability events. **Example:** Flash flooding is high risk and high probability. **Solution:** Locate EOC on high ground on the same side of the river as the normal workplaces of key personnel.
Key personnel can walk to the EOC if necessary.	Locate EOC where key personnel can walk if necessary to minimize operational delays. Traffic disruption occurs with incidents of the size, complexity, and severity that require EOC activation.
New threats pose risk to the EOC.	Consider effect on EOC with any revision of hazard/vulnerability analysis. New threats include terrorist acts and construction of high-rise buildings that could collapse in an earthquake.

Safety

Is the EOC in a safe location? Consider:

- Is the EOC location safe from natural and other hazards?
- Is the EOC location safe from high-risk cascading events?
- Is the EOC not located near a potential terrorist target?
- Can personnel walk safely to report to the EOC?
- Can personnel walk safely for meals and other amenities during EOC operations?

Other important EOC safety issues include:

- Compliance with the Americans with Disabilities Act (ADA).
- Removal of dangerous substances (i.e., asbestos).
- Ensuring appropriate security for EOC staff and visitors.
- Compliance with building codes.

Size - Key Points to Consider

The number of staff members needed at any one time	The EOC needs to accommodate the maximum number of staff members required for large, complex emergencies. **Rule of thumb:** Allow between 50 and 85 square feet per staff member. This space allowance includes working, walking, and meeting areas.
The equipment the staff will use on the job	Space planning must include room for electronic equipment, file storage, maps, and any special equipment staff members need for EOC operations.
How the equipment is configured	Consider operational requirements: needed line of sight, private communications, operational security, work groups. The optimum configuration for operations is not always the most space-efficient.
Additional equipment required to ensure interoperability and redundancy	Do current communications and information management systems have "plug and play" interoperability? If not, additional equipment must be planned for in the EOC.
Additional space for conferences, eating and sleeping, and other identified uses	Designate space (away from the noise of emergency operations) for private meetings and conferences. Staff working during extended operations require space for non-work needs.

Dealing With a Too-Small EOC

What if the EOC is too small to accommodate all your operational needs?

Here are some options:

- **Look at the entire MACS.** In a large disaster, many States coordinate the provision of mutual aid from the State EOC. Some key personnel may be deployed to another EOC. Identify, through exercises, areas in which changes in procedures and protocols could improve coordination among State and local EOCs.
- **Consider the use of Department EOCs (DEOCs).** First-response agencies use department EOCs in conjunction with dispatch for day-to-day operations. Some Department personnel may operate from DEOCs, reporting to key personnel at

the EOC. Special consideration is needed to ensure rapid communications and data transfer capability.

Systems Capability

The EOC must be capable of sustaining operations for an extended period of time. The critical requirements for systems capability include:

- **Heating, ventilation, and air conditioning (HVAC).** The HVAC system must be able to operate adequately under load with the maximum number of personnel and equipment operating at the EOC.
- **Water.** The EOC should have a dedicated water source, whenever possible.
- **Electricity.** The EOC **must** have an emergency electricity generation capability and an uninterruptible power supply (UPS) in case of a power outage in the surrounding area. Backup generators should be tested, under load, at least monthly.
- **Telephone.** An interoperable backup means of voice communications is a necessity.

Survivability

Survivability means that the EOC can remain operational for an extended period of time regardless of:

- The type, size, or complexity of the incident.
- Other damage to the surrounding infrastructure.

Survivability is the culmination of all factors in the EOC location and design.

Alternate EOCs

Continuity of operations is what distinguishes the EOC. Damage to the EOC does not absolve the jurisdiction of its coordination responsibilities, or its responsibilities for protecting the public. All jurisdictions need to identify alternate EOC locations.

The selection of an alternate EOC location should be based on the same factors as for the primary EOC.

Because the alternate EOC is designated for use only when the primary EOC is unusable, jurisdictions may choose not to equip the facility fully.

Alternate EOCs

A decision jurisdictions make when designating an alternate EOC is how to maintain the facility—hot, warm, or cold.

Hot facilities can be used as soon as personnel arrive. Hot facilities are the most expensive to maintain. They require duplicate systems and equipment, and the ongoing payment of utilities.

Warm facilities have critical systems and equipment in place. The EOC can be up and running as soon as utilities and telephones are turned on, computers are installed, etc.

Cold facilities are basically empty shells. There are no systems and equipment in place and no arrangements for utilities. Cold facilities require the longest period of time for startup.

If your jurisdiction cannot afford alternate facilities, consider a mutual aid agreement with a neighboring jurisdiction to use its EOC in the event of an emergency that renders your primary EOC unusable.

Lesson 7: Activating and Deactivating the EOC

Lesson Objectives

At the completion of this lesson, you should be able to:

- Determine when, how, and by whom the EOC will be activated.
- Define "time-phased" activation and determine when it might be appropriate.
- Analyze incident needs to determine if EOC staffing should be increased or decreased.
- Determine when and how to deactivate the EOC.

Activating the EOC

Jurisdiction policy determines EOC activation. Listed below are possible circumstances that would trigger an EOC activation.

- A Unified Command or Area Command is established.
- More than one jurisdiction becomes involved in a response.
- The Incident Commander indicates an incident could expand rapidly or involve cascading events.
- A similar incident in the past required EOC activation.
- The Chief Executive Officer (CEO) directs that the EOC should be activated.
- An emergency is imminent… hurricane warnings, slow river flooding, predictions of hazardous weather, elevated threat levels.
- Threshold events described in the Emergency Operations Plan (EOP) occur.

The Decisionmaking Process for Activation

All personnel need to be aware of:

- **Who** makes the decision to activate the EOC.
- **What** are the circumstances for activation.
- **When** activation occurs.
- **How** the level of activation is determined.

The decisionmaking process for EOC activation should be documented in policy.

Activating the EOC: Authority

Emergency Function (EF) 1
MANAGING EMERGENCY OPERATIONS

The Emergency Management Agency (EMA) is the county's 24-hour "crisis monitor." **As emergency situations threaten to occur**, the county **EMA Coordinator** may convene a "Crisis Action Team (CAT)" or **activate the Emergency Operations Center (EOC)** to facilitate evaluation and incident planning and possible activation and implementation of emergency functions and resources. Certain near instantaneous events may trigger immediate, full EOC activation. The EOC is the key to successful response and recovery operations. With decisionmakers and policymakers located together, personnel and resources can be used efficiently. Coordination of activities will ensure that all tasks are accomplished and minimize duplication of efforts.

(Excerpted from Jefferson County, AL EOP)

Note that this example of a **Managing Emergency Operations** statement clearly **indicates**:

- **Who** has the authority to activate the EOC.
- **What** are the circumstances under which the EOC is activated.

Activating the EOC: Concept of Operations

The **Concept of Operations** document for this jurisdiction supports its policy statement for EOC activation. Review the example below as a model for your jurisdiction.

IV.   CONCEPT OF OPERATIONS
        A.   GENERAL
             1.   The County Emergency Management Agency (EMA) is the lead agency for facilitating coordination among local, State, Federal, and private-sector agencies and groups within the county.
             2.   The EMA Coordinator serves as the key element in emergency planning and is the primary coordinator/advisor for the Emergency Management Council.

3. The EMA Coordinator or designee is the point of contact (POC) for State assistance.
4. During a full EOC activation, all EOC representatives are expected to coordinate directly with their functional counterparts in the local/State/Federal government and private sector.

(Excerpted from Jefferson County, AL EOP)

Activating the EOC: Roles and Responsibilities

This section, describing the EOC, clearly defines the role of the EOC and the EMA Coordinator.

D. Emergency Operations Center (EOC)

1. On behalf of the Emergency Management Council, the EMA Coordinator has the responsibility for coordinating the entire emergency management organization. The Coordinator makes all routine decisions and advises the officials on courses of action available for major decisions. During emergency operations, the Coordinator is responsible for the proper functioning of the EOC. The Coordinator also acts as a liaison with the State and Federal emergency agencies and neighboring counties.
2. The EOC is the central point for emergency management operations….Coordination and supervision of all services will be through the EOC Manager and Section Chiefs to provide for the most efficient management of resources.
3. During emergency situations, certain agencies will be required to relocate their center of control to the EOC. During large-scale emergencies, the EOC will become the seat of government for the duration of the crisis….

(Excerpted from Jefferson County, AL EOP)

Under this policy, the EMA Coordinator has the responsibility and authority for managing the county's emergency management organization and the EOC during an emergency or disaster.

Determining When the EOC Should Be Activated

Timing of EOC activation depends on the nature of the incident. Many jurisdictions have phases of EOC activation.

Time-phased activation is appropriate:

- When an incident occurs that is expected to build over time, such as wildfire.
- When there is a warning period before an emergency, such as when a hurricane or riverine flooding has been forecast.
- In preparation for planned events.

Time-Phased Activation

Consider these Activation Phases.

- Level 1 (Full): All personnel
- Level 2 (Partial): Key personnel and personnel from responding agencies
- Level 3 (Monitor): Key personnel only

Determining the Level of Activation

The level of EOC activation should be based on established **triggers** and **communication** with the Incident Commander or Unified Command.

Link levels of activation to the jurisdiction's Hazard Analysis. The Hazard Analysis then helps define **triggers** for activation, based on actual or anticipated levels of damage.

Communication between the Incident Commander (or Unified Command) and the EOC is a critical element of an activation decision. On-scene command has the most up-to-date information about the on-scene situation, knows whether the situation is under control, and is aware of incident needs.

Deactivating the EOC

The on-scene commander is aware of the current incident status and knows:

- What remains to be done.

- What resources are required to meet the incident objectives.
- How long it will take to meet incident objectives.
- When the demand for resources slows down.

Consider recovery needs. Often, the EOC must remain activated to facilitate recovery needs after the Incident Command completes its on-scene mission.

Deactivating the EOC

The decisionmaker for deactivating EOC functions will vary by jurisdiction. In most cases, the Emergency Management Coordinator will make the decision jointly with agency key personnel and jurisdiction leaders.

EOC decisionmakers should make the decision when to release personnel and other resources only after discussion with on-scene commanders.

The authority to begin full or partial deactivation should be clearly stated in the jurisdiction's EOP, and all personnel should know:

- Who has the authority.
- The process that will be followed for deactivation.

Recommendation: Deactivate in phases. It is more efficient and cost effective to deactivate personnel as they are no longer needed.

Post-Incident Evaluation

EOC operations should be evaluated after every activation, and every aspect of operations should be evaluated. The persons listed below should be included in the evaluation process:

- **All key EOC personnel.**
- The **Incident Commander(s).**
- **Jurisdiction leadership** or their designees who were involved at the EOC.
- Others as appropriate under the circumstances, such as utility company representatives, members of the media, and representatives from nongovernmental organizations.

After-Action Analysis and Reporting Process

As a minimum, the following activities should be included as part of after-action analysis and reporting:

- Report EOC performance completely.
- Develop solutions, rather than merely listing problems.
- Develop a plan to train, test, and exercise the proposed solutions.
- Carry after-action results over to the EOP.

Recommendation: Adopt a "nonattribution rule" to encourage open and honest discussion of what worked well and what didn't.

Lesson 8: EOC Operations

Lesson Objectives

At the completion of this lesson, you should be able to:

- Describe the attributes of an effective ICS/EOC interface.
- Develop strategies to resolve common operational problems at the EOC.
- List the physical, cognitive, and behavioral signs of stress.
- Provide effective psychological support to EOC staff.

EOC Function Review: Large, Complex Incidents

During large, complex incidents the EOC assumes a coordination role. As an incident expands in size or increases in complexity, central coordination is needed, and provided by the EOC.

The point of overlap—the ICS/EOC interface—is usually the area of disconnect in emergency planning.

EOC Function Review

The most common ICS/EOC interface issues center around communications, SOPs, resource management, and personnel training. Communication and Information Management concerns were covered in an earlier lesson. This topic will address SOPs, resource management, and personnel training.

SOPs

Develop Standard Operating Procedures for **every** EOC position. Be sure to include:

- What is required of the position.
- When the SOP is effective.
- The timeframe for mobilization, operations, and demobilization.
- When the SOP is no longer effective.

SOP Development and Update

EOC SOP development is a team responsibility. The Emergency Management Coordinator and each function head should jointly compose the SOPs.

EOC SOPs should be:

- Developed as part of the planning process.
- Reviewed and revised after each activation or exercise, or annually.

Resource Management

Resource management can be an area of confusion between the on-scene command structure and the EOC. As shown in the table below, however, the role of the EOC complements that of the ICS structure.

Compare resource management at the Command Post versus the EOC:

Command Post	EOC
Identify needs	Receive requests
Order resources	Prioritize requests
Check in resources	Locate/order resources
Assign resources	Assign according to priorities
Track resources	Track resource use
Demobilize resources	Pay for resources

The on-scene command structure manages resources based on:

- Complete incident sizeup.
- Subsequent incident objectives.
- Tactics.

The principles of ICS ensure an orderly approach to identifying incident resource needs.

When incidents grow in size and/or complexity and more tactical resources are required, the EOC and the entire multiagency coordination system (MACS) play an increasingly important role in resource management.

Switching Resource Ordering to the EOC

One common issue around resource managers is the question of when the Incident Commander should request resources from the EOC rather than from the dispatch center. Many jurisdictions have established triggers to help the Incident Commander make that decision. Possible triggers are shown in the table below.

Activation of the EOC	Some jurisdictions automatically switch their resource ordering and tracking to the EOC as soon as it is fully operational.
Dispatch workload increases beyond specified threshold	The call load for dispatch rises as an incident expands. Dispatch may reach a point where it cannot provide dispatch services and/or cannot provide large-incident logistical support.
Establishment of a Unified Command or Area Command	Multiple agencies with shared responsibility for a response, or multiple incidents with separate Incident Command structures, will need resource management from the EOC.
Normal mutual aid resources are exhausted	There is a need for increased delegation of authority to commit finances.

To help all personnel recognize triggers for switching resource ordering to the EOC, the process should be:

- Stated clearly in the jurisdiction's Emergency Operations Plan.
- Implemented through the jurisdiction's chain of command.
- Supported by dependable communications.

The procedures for switching resource ordering to the EOC should be trained and exercised regularly.

Staffing the EOC

Planning for EOC staffing is a critical aspect of EOC management and operations. There is a tendency to overstaff day-to-day EOC operations. The staffing equivalents shown in the table below are a reasonable "rule of thumb" for day-to-day EOC staffing.

Population	Full-Time Equivalent Staff
Over 1,000,000	6 – 20
250,000 to 1,000,000	4 – 8

100,000 to 250,000	3 – 5
25,000 to 100,000	2 – 3
Under 25,000	1 – 2

Day-To-Day Staffing

What functions are covered in the EOC day to day? Although day-to-day functions vary among jurisdictions of various sizes and threat levels, minimal day-to-day functions include:

- Emergency Management.
- Communications.
- Public Information.
- Finance and Administration.
- Logistics.
- Security.

There may be additional functions needed for your EOC. One staff person may have responsibilities for multiple functions.

Emergency Staffing

EOC staffing should expand and contract with the needs of the emergency.

Larger and/or more complex incidents will require a greater level of activation and a larger number of staff.

At full activation, most staff members will be assigned responsibility for only one function or position.

Ensuring Qualified Staff

The Emergency Management Coordinator may **not** have control over assignment of staff, but does have direct control over the training of emergency management staff. Working closely with key personnel from other agencies can ensure that staff members are fully qualified for the jobs to which they are assigned.

Some ways to facilitate the training process include:

Developing position descriptions (PDs) for every position.	<ul><li>PDs provide a list of the general responsibilities for each EOC position.</li><li>PDs serve as a good starting point for determining training needs.</li></ul>
Developing an overall training strategy.	Work with other agency key personnel to create orientations, classroom training, on-the-job training, and a mentoring program.
Providing training opportunities on common tasks.	Consolidate training needs for personnel from the multiple agencies represented in the EOC.
Using information from exercises and actual operations.	Prior experience, as noted in after-action reports, is a guideline for the skills and knowledge that require training.

Consider cross-training for specific positions to ensure that all critical tasks are covered by qualified staff.

Coordinating With Other Parts of the MACS

Typically coordination with other parts of the MACS occurs when:

- **Mutual aid is requested.** The provision of mutual aid is a trigger for coordination between or among the EOCs of the jurisdictions involved.
- **Technical specialists are required.** The provision of technical specialists, such as those provided by State environmental agencies, research universities, and/or outside contractors, often triggers coordination between MAC entities.
- **The emergency is widespread or a Federal disaster is declared.** Widespread emergencies or federally declared disasters automatically trigger the activation of MAC elements and entities.

The most common coordination point with other parts of the MACS is when external assistance is needed. A model process for requesting external assistance is shown below.

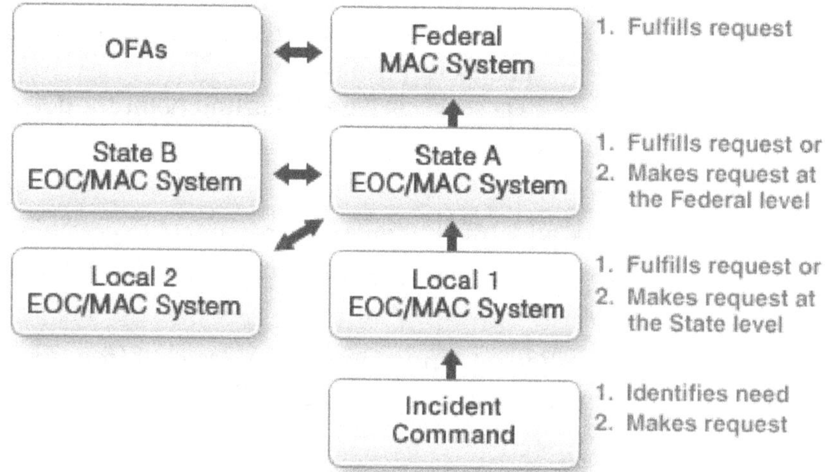

In this model, all requests for mutual aid at the local level are processed through the State. Resource orders to the next higher level of government may first need a **formal request for assistance**.

Requesting Assistance Within the MACS

When requesting assistance from another part of the MACS, it is important to make the request as complete as possible. All requests should be made formally and include:

- The type of incident.
- The time the incident occurred (or is expected to occur).
- Actions already taken.
- Areas and number of people involved.
- Estimates of loss of life, injuries, and extent of damage.
- The type and amount of assistance required.
- The time and place for delivery.
- A contact for followup questions.

A formal request for assistance should always be followed up by the actual **resource order.** The resource order provides detailed information on the **kind** and **type** of resource that is needed—what, where, and when.

Tips for Requesting External Assistance

When requesting assistance:

- Ask sooner rather than later. Coordination takes time. There will be some delay between the time that a resource is requested and the time it arrives and can be assigned.
- Make all resource requests based on the mission, task, incident objectives, and established priorities.
- Follow established procedures for requesting external resources to ensure that the resource assignments can be made and tracked accurately.

Long-Term Issues

Common long-term issues at the EOC include documentation, resources, staffing, and costs.

Long-term operations usually equate to more damage or damage over an extended area. Plans need to include strategies for ensuring proper **documentation** of damage, the resources used, equipment maintenance performed, overtime hours, etc.

Long-term operations take their toll on incident **resources**. Human **resources** need to rotate out of service to eat and rest. Mechanical **resources** require refueling or maintenance. Careful coordination between the Incident Command and the EOC is needed to ensure there are enough resources on-scene and in the staging area for response operations to continue without interruption.

EOC staff need to eat, rest, and decompress during long-term operations. EOC **staffing** patterns should include enough personnel to ensure 24-hour coverage for extended EOC operations, including backup coverage. If necessary, staffing should be augmented through mutual aid agreements with other jurisdictions and levels of government.

Long-term operations equate to higher **costs**. It is not unusual for jurisdictions to expend their entire year's overtime budgets for a single long-term incident. The terms of intergovernmental agreements may include provisions for payment if an incident extends past an agreed-upon threshold. Add the costs of the response to the financial impact of damage to public infrastructure and resources, and the financial effects can be as catastrophic as the disaster itself.

Resolving Long-Term Issues

When the incident is expected to last more than one operational period, or when the EOC is expected to be activated for an extended period, issues will invariably arise. Follow these strategies to resolve long-term issues:

- Describe detailed agency staffing requirements in the EOP.
- Verify all agencies have fulfilled the EOP staffing requirements.
- Conduct exercises to verify resources, staffing, and documentation systems are adequate for long-term operations.
- Develop recordkeeping system to record costs, damage, staffing, and equipment use at the scene and at the EOC.

One important way to resolve issues is to ensure that all key decisionmakers are at the EOC. **Having all key personnel in one place facilitates discussion and rapid problemsolving as issues arise.**

Senior personnel from the jurisdiction(s) need to be involved at the EOC and need to have the authority to make binding decisions in the moment.

When Mediation Becomes Necessary

During long-term operations, disagreements are bound to occur, and some will not be resolved easily. It may be necessary for the Emergency Management Coordinator or another senior official to **mediate** the disagreement. When mediation becomes necessary, it is vital that the mediator:

Suspend judgment on the issue at hand.	Even if the mediator has an opinion about how the situation should be handled, the issue cannot be mediated if he or she allows that opinion to influence the discussion.
Listen carefully to both sides of the discussion.	The mediator should verify that he or she understands what has been said by reflecting back the conversation using his or her own words.
Analyze the discussion and make suggestions.	After listening to the discussion, the mediator should make suggestions that will satisfy the needs of both sides to the degree possible.

Be careful not to make suggestions sound like the solution is obvious or that the decision has already been made.

Maintaining a Positive Climate

The EOC can be a pressure cooker, especially during long-term operations. Tension is inherent in the environment. Although it may not be possible to prevent tension, there are actions that Emergency Management Coordinators can take to mitigate it.

Over the short term, moderate stress can be a motivator, but over an extended period, high levels of stress can be debilitating personally and dysfunctional organizationally.

Resolving High Stress Levels Before EOC Operations

Depending on the incident, stress levels among EOC staff may begin to rise even before activation. High stress levels before operations must be managed early before they interfere with operations.

One of the best ways to reduce preoperational stress levels is to ensure that all positions are well documented and that staff are trained and exercised in their job tasks. Other steps for managing stress before operations begin are shown in the table below.

Look for opportunities to become a team.	Team building can occur during training and exercises.
Schedule briefings to talk about how experienced personnel have dealt with stress.	Help staff identify signs of stress. Providing useful techniques for reducing stress will help everyone during operations.

Resolving High Stress Levels During EOC Operations

Stress levels naturally increase during EOC operations. Too much stress can cause mistakes, however, and mistakes at the EOC can cause injury or death at the scene.

Two ways to identify and alleviate high stress levels during operations are shown in the table below.

Encourage personnel to take breaks away from their desks and to get rest when the opportunity arises.	Promote good eating habits and exercise.

| Be alert to behavior changes, such as irritability or the inability to make decisions. | Act sooner, rather than later. Don't wait until an individual is unable to function. |

Managing Stress After Operations

Stress doesn't end when EOC operations end. In fact, some people who perform in an exemplary way during operations may experience unbearable stress when operations are curtailed. Some ways to identify and alleviate stress levels following operations are shown in the table below. If necessary, professional counseling and other services should be made available to those who can benefit from them.

Conduct stress debriefings.	Debrief when personnel are demobilized and several days after returning to their day-to-day jobs.
Follow up over time to ensure that personnel are coping effectively.	Have a casual conversation, or observe as the person completes daily job tasks.
Involve other people, especially managers and those who know and care about the person.	The ability to talk through a troubling situation with a trusted friend is often helpful for resolving personal conflict and reducing stress.
Provide professional help, if necessary.	Professional help is often provided to responders at the scene but may be forgotten for those in the EOC.

Stress and Decisionmaking

The EOC environment has a great effect on decisionmaking. As a result of the stressors in the EOC, decisionmakers are more likely to:

- Experience conflict with others.
- Perceive selectively because of sensory overload and miss important information.
- Experience perception distortion and poor judgment.

Characteristics of decisionmakers experiencing prolonged stress include:

- Less tolerance of ambiguity, resulting in premature decisions.
- More difficulty handling demanding tasks.
- Greater tendency toward aggression.
- Tunnel vision.

Improving Decisionmaking When Under Stress

- **Establish a routine** in the EOC and follow it. This ensures that specified tasks occur in the same way to the degree possible. Focus can then be extended to "nonroutine" tasks.
- **Adopt a decisionmaking model**. These generally follow the same steps:
  1. Identify the problem or issue.
  2. Explore possible solutions.
  3. Narrow possible solutions.
  4. Select the solution that provides the best option.

Lesson 9: Tests, Training, and Exercises EOC Operations

Lesson Objectives

At the completion of this lesson, you should be able to:

- Define the terms test, training, and exercise.
- Explain how tests, training, and exercises are used to ensure effective EOC operations.
- Describe the Homeland Security Exercise and Evaluation Program (HSEEP).
- Select the type(s) of tests, training, and exercises that are appropriate to a given scenario.

Tests, Training, and Exercises (TT&E) Defined

TT&E for EOC operations can be defined as:

Measures taken to ensure that a jurisdiction's EOC is capable of supporting response and recovery throughout an incident period.

This is not an official definition, but it does explain the main goal of TT&E for EOCs.

TT&E as an Integrated Program

TT&E events should be conducted as part of an overall program.

- Ensure that all TT&E events share the common overall goal of mission readiness.
- Provide a framework for readiness activities that will ensure consistency and uniformity.

A well-planned and developed **TT&E program** helps ensure that TT&E events are consistent, progressive, and focused on common goals that will complement and build on each other.

An Effective TT&E Program

Effective TT&E programs share several common attributes.

- TT&E programs provide training in the appropriate functional areas of mission readiness.
- TT&E programs allow EOC personnel to apply the skills and knowledge they gained in training.
- TT&E programs build team unity through meaningful opportunities for team members to work together.

Goal of TT&E: Mission Readiness

The TT&E program should blend testing, training, and exercise events to ensure personnel interest levels are maintained and all bases covered. Information presented should be current and credible!

To achieve the goal of **mission readiness**, the TT&E program should:

- Consist of all three components—tests, training, and exercises.
- Reflect lessons learned from previous TT&E events and actual emergencies.

Tests

Tests are conducted to evaluate **capabilities**, not personnel. From an emergency operations perspective, tests are an excellent way to evaluate:

- Communications.
- Alert and notification processes.
- Deployment.

Training

Training is instruction in core competencies and skills. It is the principal means by which individuals achieve a level of proficiency. Typically, a significant part of the TT&E program will involve training.

Training provides the tools needed to:

- Accomplish a goal.
- Meet program requirements.
- Acquire a specified capability.

Training encompasses a range of activities with a common purpose, including:

- To provide information, or
- To refine skills.

Exercises

Exercises are events that allow participants to apply their skills and knowledge to improve operational readiness.

Planners use exercises to evaluate effectiveness of simulations and tests.

The primary purpose of an exercise is to identify areas that require additional training, planning, or other resources to improve the jurisdiction's mission capability.

An exercise can determine if:

- Policies and procedures are effective.
- Training is up to standards.
- Adequate resources are available.

HSEEP

The importance of exercises hit home after the terrorist attacks of 1995 and 2001. FEMA's Preparedness Directorate in DHS is responsible for managing and updating HSEEP.

HSEEP:

- Provides common exercise policy and program guidance.
- Is a national standard for homeland security exercises.
- Uses consistent terminology that can be used by all exercise planners.

HSEEP Concepts

HSEEP reflects lessons learned and best practices of existing exercise programs. It integrates language and concepts from the:

- National Incident Management System
- National Response Framework

HSEEP is appropriate for all hazards. FEMA's and EMI's curricula are now based on the HSEEP model.

HSEEP Strategy

Homeland Security Presidential Directive (HSPD) 5 directed DHS to coordinate the development of:

- A National Incident Management System (NIMS).
- The National Response Framework (NRF).

HSPD-8 directed DHS to coordinate the development of the Homeland Security Exercise and Evaluation Program.

HSEEP provides the Nation with a common, consistent platform for its homeland security exercise needs.

The NRP has been superseded by the National Framework Framework (NRF), which improves coordination among responding agencies.

HSEEP Exercise Types

HSEEP has two broad categories of exercises based on the level of fidelity, stress induced, and other factors. These categories are:

- Discussion-based—seminars, workshops, tabletop exercises, and games.
- Operations-based—drills, functional exercises, and full-scale exercises.

HSEEP: A Blended Approach

HSEEP facilitates the creation of self-sustaining, capabilities-based exercise programs by providing program management resources for:

- Policy and Guidance.
- Training.
- Technology.
- Support.

By using a blended approach, HSEEP ensures that jurisdictions at all levels of government have the tools they need to implement their doctrine and policy successfully.

The Universal Task List (UTL) and the Target Capabilities List (TCL) are capabilities-based planning tools developed to fulfill that need.

Universal Task List (UTL):
The UTL is a comprehensive menu of tasks derived from all tasks that may be performed in major incidents as illustrated by the National Planning Scenarios. Entities at all levels of government should use the UTL as a reference to help them develop proficiency through training and exercises to perform their assigned missions and tasks during major incidents.

Target Capabilities List (TCL):
The TCL is a list of capabilities that provides guidance on the specific capabilities that Federal, State, tribal, and local entities are expected to develop and maintain to prevent, protect against, respond to, and recover from incidents.

Benefits of a Capabilities-Based Exercise Program

There are three main benefits to a capabilities-based exercise program:

- Personnel have an opportunity to practice their roles and responsibilities.
- Jurisdictions can measure their actual capabilities in specified areas.
- Jurisdictions can improve their overall emergency management systems.

Value of Exercises

Benefits arise not only from the exercises, but from evaluating the exercises and acting on the lessons learned. Exercises have value only when they lead to improvement.

The focus of any exercise should be to identify and eliminate problems **before** an actual emergency occurs. Corrective actions are an important part of exercise design, evaluation, and followup.

Additional Benefits of Exercises

Additional benefits of exercises include:

- Identification of planning weaknesses.
- Improved coordination and communication.
- Clarification of roles and responsibilities.
- Identification of resource gaps.
- Public support and confidence in the jurisdiction's ability to respond to emergencies.

The **TT&E Event Checklist**, adapted from COOP, is a useful guide for planning a TT&E event.